HOW IT ALL BEGAN...

SMOKE ON THE MOUNTAIN was first produced in 1988 at the McCarter Theatre in Princeton, New Jersey, and went on to a 500-performance run at New York's Lamb's Theatre, becoming the longest-running production in the history of that theatre. During its New York engagement, SMOKE ON THE MOUNTAIN received award nominations from the Drama Desk, Outer Critics Circle and Stage Directors and Choreographers Foundation. Additionally, it was named one of the best plays of the year by various publications, including *Time* magazine, *The New York Times*, the Associated Press, *The New York Post*, and *New York Newsday*.

Following its New York run, SMOKE ON THE MOUNTAIN has gone on to gross more than $60 million across the country. Long-running productions include Atlanta, Nashville, Branson, Seattle, and San Francisco and such major cities as Chicago, Houston, Boston, Cincinnati, St. Louis, Phoenix, Detroit, San Diego, Kansas City, Richmond, Sarasota, and Little Rock. Internationally, SMOKE ON THE MOUNTAIN has been presented in England, Ireland, Canada, Australia, and New Zealand.

SMOKE ON THE MOUNTAIN is currently the most frequently-licensed title in the catalog of Samuel French, Inc., the world's largest and foremost publisher of plays. SMOKE ON THE MOUNTAIN's sequels, SANDERS FAMILY CHRISTMAS and SMOKE ON THE MOUNTAIN HOMECOMING, are also among the most-licensed plays in Samuel French's catalog.

An impressive resume for "the little show that could!"

Tommy Hancock (Burl), Rhonda Wallace (Vera) and Jeremy Aggers (Dennis) are interrupted by Ross Schexnayder (Mervin) in CCP's 2005 **Smoke on the Mountain**
Photo: Tracy Knauss
Cumberland County Playho▮

Denise and Dennis Sanders
Smoke on the Mountain
Theatre in the Square, Marietta, Georgia

Vera, Burl and Stanley Sanders
Smoke on the Mountain
Theatre in the Square, Marietta, Georgia

Smoke on the Mountain

NEW AND CLASSIC GOSPEL SONGS

WRITTEN BY CONNIE RAY

CONCEIVED BY ALAN BAILEY

ARRANGEMENTS BY MIKE CRAVER AND MARK HARDWICK

Shawnee Press, Inc.
A Subsidiary of Music Sales Corporation
1221 17th Avenue South · Nashville, TN 37212

Visit Shawnee Press Online at www.shawneepress.com/songbooks

SB1029

CONTENTS

Rock of Ages

AUGUSTUS M. TOPLADY, 1775

THOMAS HASTINGS, 1832

The Church in the Wildwood

Words and Music by
DR. WILLIAM S. PITTS, 1865

A Wonderful Time Up There
(Everybody's Gonna Have a Wonderful Time Up There)

Words and Music by
LEE ROY ABERNATHY

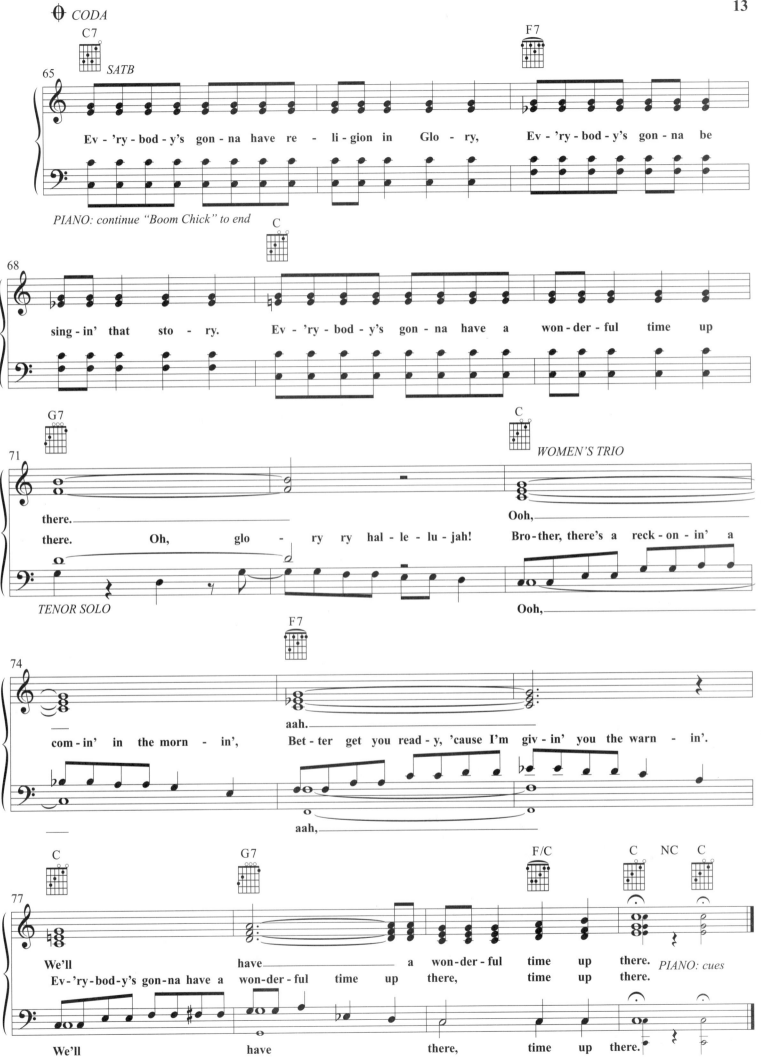

No Tears in Heaven

Words and Music by
ROBERT S. ARNOLD

1st time: SOLO (top notes)
2nd time: TRIO

1. No tears in Heav-en, no sor-row giv-en, All will be glo-ry in that
2. Glo-ry is wait-ing, wait-ing up yon-der where we shall spend an end-less

PIANO: R.H. upstems, L.H. downstems (bass clef)

1st time: DUET (top and bottom notes)

land; There'll be no sad-ness, all will be glad-ness
day. There with our Sav-ior we'll be for-ev-er,

when we shall join that hap-py band.
where no more sor-row can dis-may.

Smoke on the Mountain
Totem Pole Playhouse,
Caledonia State Park,
Fayetteville, PA

Smoke on the Mountain
Full cast, from left to right:
Laura Floyd as Denise,
Alan Kilpatrick as Rev. Mervin
Oglethorpe, Karen Howell as Vera,
J. P. Peterson as Burl, Jennifer Akin
as June, Scott DePoy as Stanley
and Travis Smith as Dennis

Theatre in the Square,
Marietta, Georgia

Photo: M. J. Conboy

Smoke on the Mountain
Totem Pole Playhouse,
Caledonia State Park,
Fayetteville, PA

The Filling Station

Words and Music by
APRIL ANNE NYE

2nd time to Coda

shout.___ Ev - 'ry - thing is free, it - 'll nev - er run out at the fill - in'___ sta - tion._____

PIANO: play cues

TENOR SOLO

2. I can see the world a trem - blin' and a search - in',___ a look - in' for an an - swer that is cer - tain.___ It's up to us___ to share___ God's love with

PIANO: R.H. upstems, L.H. downstems (bass clef)

I'll Never Die
(I'll Just Change My Address)

Words and Music by
J. PRESTON MARTINEZ

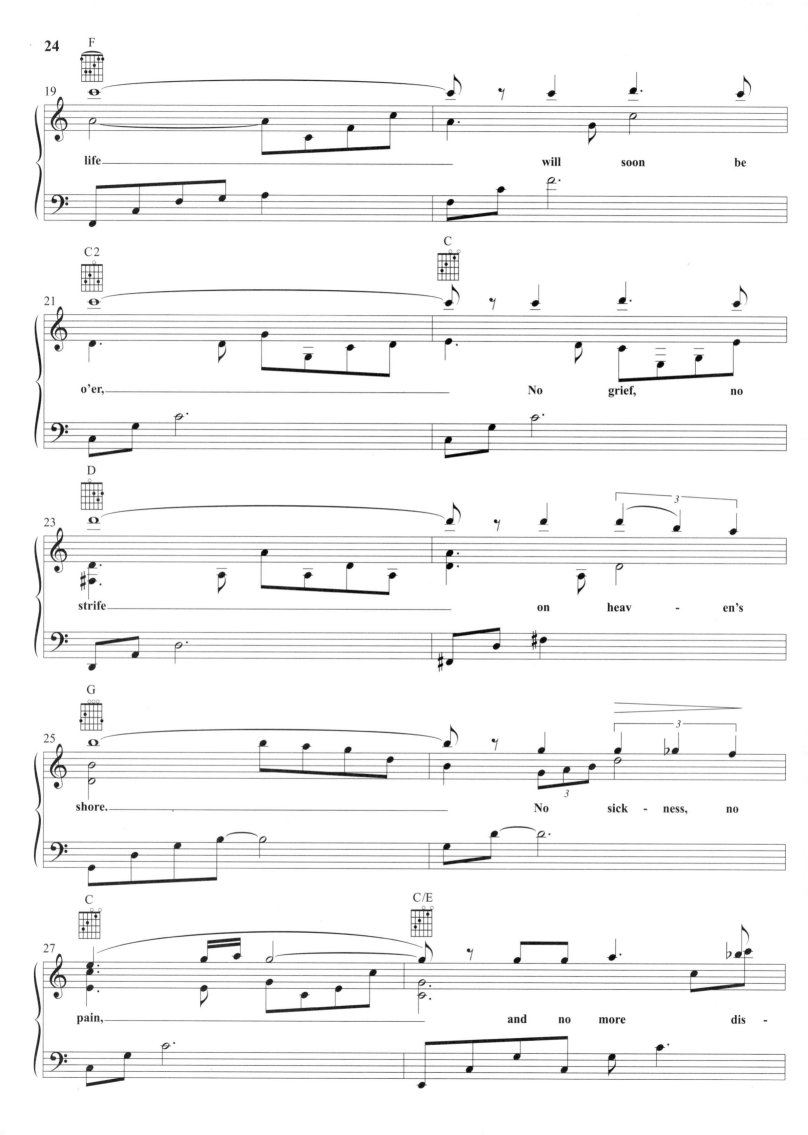

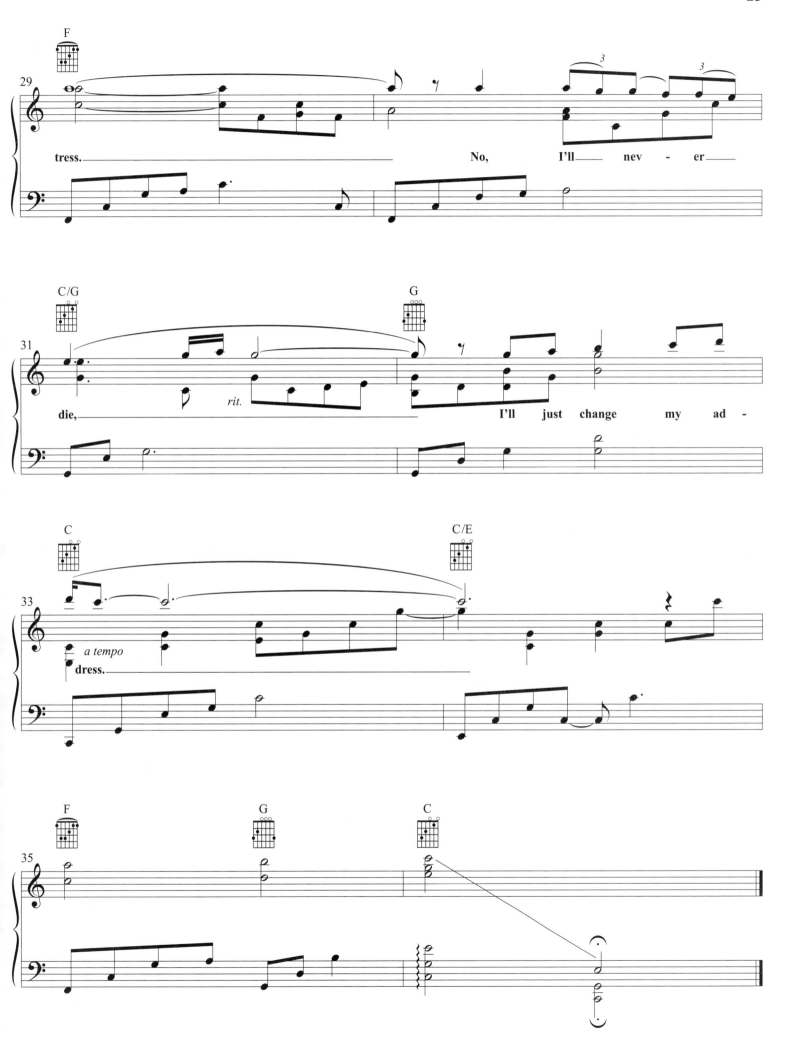

Jesus Is Mine

Words and Music by
WALLY FOWLER *and* **VIRGINIA STOUT COOK**

PIANO: R.H. upstems, L.H. downstems (bass clef)

TENOR SOLO

I'm so hap - py as I trav - el on the right road to Glo - ry - land. And I'm liv - ing so my light for Je - sus will shine.

Blood Medley

With joy and energy ♩ = 106 - 112

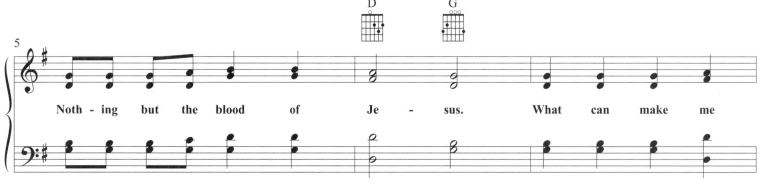

PIANO: continue "boom-chick" accompaniment

Nothing but the Blood *(Robert Lowry)*

What can wash a - way my sin?

Noth - ing but the blood of Je - sus. What can make me

whole a - gain? Noth - ing but the blood of Je - sus.

There Is Power in the Blood *(Lewis E. Jones)*

DUET: Alto and Tenor

mel.

PIANO: continue "boom-chick" accompaniment

There Is a Fountain

WILLIAM COWPER, 1731 - 1800

Early American melody

I'll Live a Million Years

Words and Music by
LEE ROY ABERNATHY

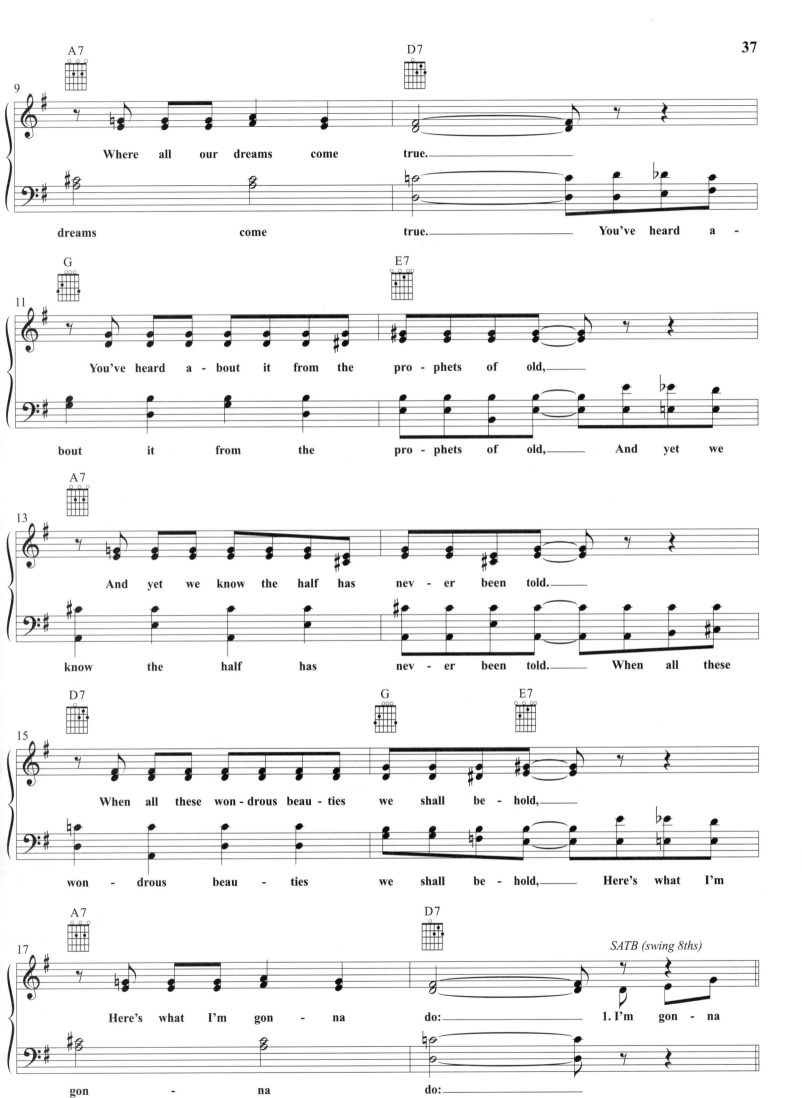

⁴⁰ I Wouldn't Take Nothing for My Journey Now

Words and Music by
JIMMIE DAVIS *and* **CHARLES F. GOODMAN**

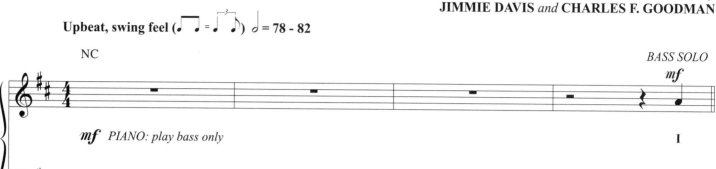

started out trav-'lin' for the Lord man-y years— a- go.   I've

had a lot-ta heart- ache,   met a lot-ta grief— and   woe.——

And   when I would stum - ble, then— I would hum - ble down,

PIANO: R.H. upstems, L.H. downstems (bass clef)

Smoke on the Mountain
Totem Pole Playhouse,
Caledonia State Park,
Fayetteville, PA

*Reverend with June Sanders
playing accordian & handbell*
Smoke on the Mountain
Theatre in the Square,
Marietta, Georgia

*Reverend with June Sanders
June signing*
Smoke on the Mountain
Theatre in the Square,
Marietta, Georgia

Angel Band

Words and Music by
J. HASCALL and **Wm. B. BRADBURY**

Moderately slow, shuffle (♩ ♪ = ♩ ♪) ♩ = 80 - 84

SOLO

mp PIANO: Play both cues and vocals

1. My

lat - est___ sun is sink - in' fast, My___ race is

near - ly___ run._____ My___ strong - est___ tri - al now is

DUET

past, My___ tri - umph is be - gun._____

Suddenly faster, straight eighths

Whispering Hope

a cappella

Words and Music by
ALICE HAWTHORNE

Tender and expressive ♩ = 90 - 94

DUET: SOP. and TEN.

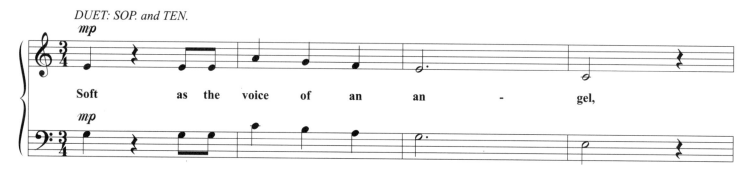

Soft as the voice of an an - gel,

Breath - ing a les - son un - heard,_____

Hope with a gen - tle per - sua - sion

Whis - pers her com - fort - ing word;_____

51

SATB

Wait   till the dark - ness is   o -   ver,

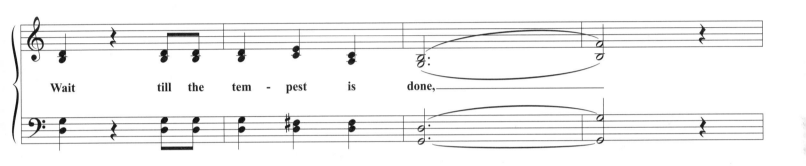

Wait   till the tem - pest is   done,_____

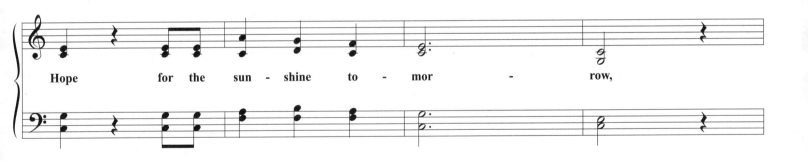

Hope   for the sun - shine to - mor -   row,

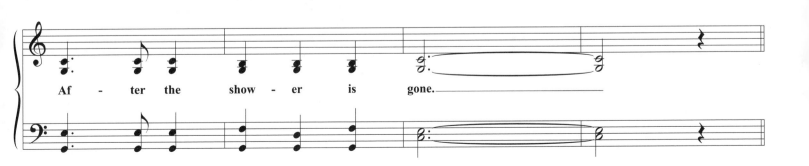

Af - ter the show - er is   gone._____

52

Smoke on the Mountain

Words and Music by
ALAN BAILEY

I'll Fly Away

Words and Music by
ALBERT E. BRUMLEY

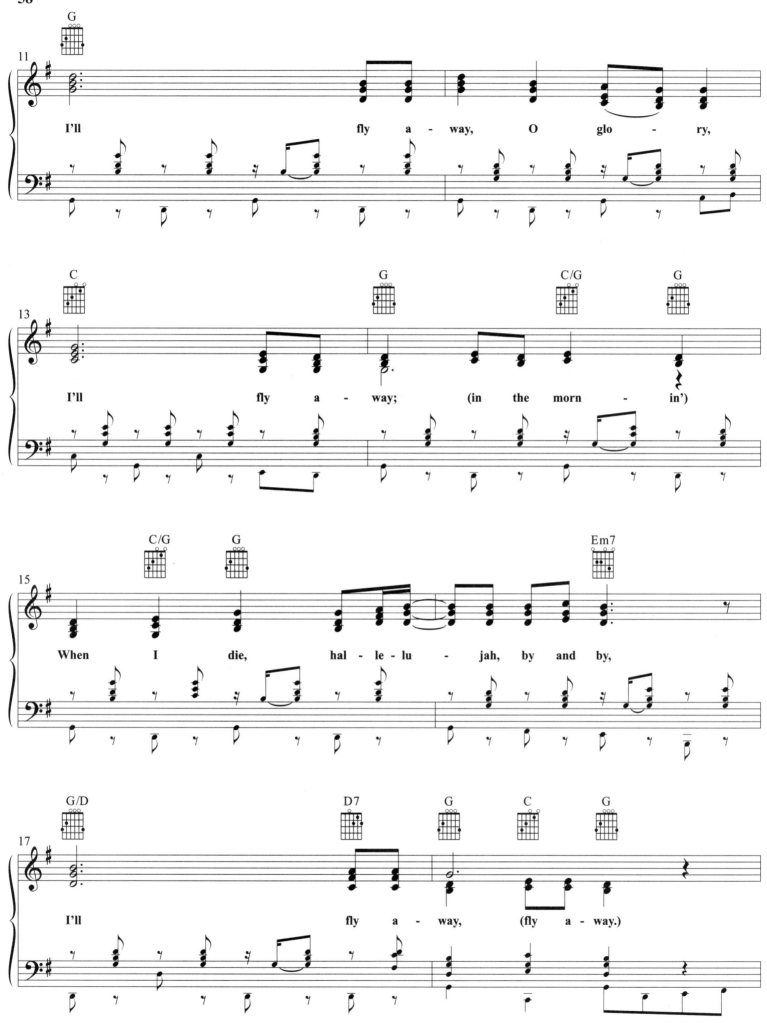

ABOUT THE CREATORS...

Connie Ray
Writer

In addition to SMOKE ON THE MOUNTAIN and its sequels SANDERS FAMILY CHRISTMAS and SMOKE ON THE MOUNTAIN HOMECOMING, Ms. Ray's plays include VANILLA TRIPLETS, CATFISH LOVES ANNA, HURTLING THROUGH SPACE, and BETSY LOVES SNAPBEANS, all produced in New York and subsequently in theaters across the country.

Ms. Ray wrote several episodes of the NBC sitcom THE TORKELSONS, in which she also starred.

Originally from North Carolina, Ms. Ray currently resides in Los Angeles.

Alan Bailey
Conceiver

Along with SMOKE ON THE MOUNTAIN, Mr. Bailey's New York writing credits include HENRY THE 8TH AT THE GRAND OLE OPRY, THE 2ND SECOND SHEPHERDS PLAY, and MOUNTAIN MOTHERS. He has written eight plays that have been produced regionally; he contributed to the scores of six of these shows.

A Georgia native, Mr. Bailey currently resides in Los Angeles. He is a five-time undefeated JEOPARDY champion.

The St. Louis Actors Ensemble celebrates its 10th Season of **Smoke on the Mountain** in Branson, MO in 2008!

ABOUT THE SHOW...

SMOKE ON THE MOUNTAIN, conceived by Alan Bailey and written by Connie Ray, tells the story of a Saturday Night Gospel Sing at a country church in North Carolina's Blue Ridge Mountains in 1938. The show features two dozen rousing bluegrass songs played and sung by the Sanders Family, a traveling group that is making their return to performing after a five-year hiatus.

Pastor Oglethorpe, the young and enthusiastic minister of Mount Pleasant Baptist Church, has enlisted the Sanders Family in his efforts to bring his tiny congregation into the "modern world." Opening night jitters — combined with the disdain of a pair of spinsters, the church's chief benefactors — keep the evening on the verge of chaos.

Between songs, each family member "witnesses" — telling a story about something important in their life. Though they try in vain to appear perfect in the eyes of a congregation who wants to be inspired by their songs, one thing after another goes awry and they reveal their true — and hilariously imperfect — natures. By the evening's end, the Sanders Family have endeared themselves to us by revealing their weaknesses and allowing us to share in their triumphs over them.

The success of SMOKE ON THE MOUNTAIN owes much to the family feeling it inspires in audiences. With warmth and humor, SMOKE ON THE MOUNTAIN makes us look fondly at the heartaches and triumphs of our own families. And with its energetic and uplifting musical score, it leaves audiences clamoring for more.

Summer Dawn Wallace
as Denise Sanders in CCP's 2005
Smoke on the Mountain

Photo: Sandra "Sam" Hahn

Cumberland County Playhouse

Left to right: Allen Cox, David
Anthony Lewis, Aubrey Bean,
Edd Key, Kevin Brady
and Loni Kappus
Smoke on the Mountain
Taproot Theatre

Photo: Eric Stuhaug

WHAT CRITICS HAVE SAID ABOUT THE SHOW...

Good ol' country folk sing the evening away in this funny, affectionate look at a Saturday night church meeting circa 1938. Praise be!

Time Magazine

A delightful revelation of the rich complexity and orneriness of people whose faith is powerful but far from unquestioning. The characters feel like a warm old-fashioned family.

New York Times

Exhilarating! The novel proceedings are constantly amusing!

Variety

The Waltons meets Seinfeld.

Next Magazine

If you want a totally beguiling entertainment, run, forget about walking, to the heartwarming SMOKE ON THE MOUNTAIN.

New York Post

It doesn't matter what church you go to, or whether you go to any church, synagogue, temple, or mosque. To fall in love with SMOKE ON THE MOUNTAIN, all you've got to be is human.

Nashville Tennessean

It's hard not to be converted by SMOKE ON THE MOUNTAIN. Your spirits are raised by the sound of small-town America singing.

San Francisco Chronicle

If having a good time at the Mount Pleasant Baptist Church is sinful, well, we are sunk.

Detroit Free Press

With its zesty combination of joy and tenderness, SMOKE ON THE MOUNTAIN is splendid and not to be missed.

Seattle Post-Intelligencer

I recommend running to SMOKE ON THE MOUNTAIN as fast as the weather will allow. You'll clap your hands, stomp your feet, laugh, and find yourself moved in the midst of your laughter.

New York Daily News

Well-nigh perfect. The audience went simply wild over SMOKE ON THE MOUNTAIN.

Philadelphia Daily News

SMOKE ON THE MOUNTAIN takes us back to simpler times where people suffered, sang, and laughed while they searched for perfection in an imperfect world.

Cincinnati Enquirer

The happiest, singin'est show in town! It's strong, comic, moving, and full of joy.

Diplomatic World Bulletin

Now that you have the printed music for

SMOKE ON THE MOUNTAIN

...Enjoy the recording!

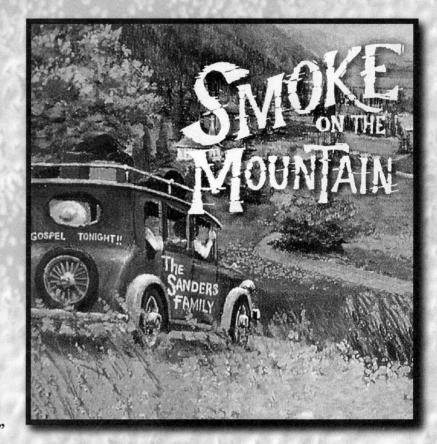

1. ROCK OF AGES
2. THE CHURCH IN THE WILDWOOD
3. A WONDERFUL TIME UP THERE
4. MEET MOTHER IN THE SKIES
5. NO TEARS IN HEAVEN
6. CHRSTIAN COWBOY
7. THE FILLING STATION
8. I'LL NEVER DIE
   (I'LL JUST CHANGE MY ADDRESS)
9. JESUS IS MINE
10. BLOOD MEDLEY
    "Nothing But the Blood Of Jesus"
    "Are You Washed In the Blood"
    "There Is Power In The Blood"
    "There Is A Fountain"
11. I'LL LIVE A MILLION YEARS
12. EVERYONE HOME BUT ME
13. I WOULDN'T TAKE NOTHIN'
    FOR MY JOURNEY NOW
14. ANGEL BAND
15. WHISPERING HOPE
16. TRANSPORTATION MEDLEY
    "I'm Using My Bible For A Roadmap"
    "I'll Walk Every Step Of The Way"
    "I'm Taking A Flight"
    "Life's Railway To Heaven"
17. SMOKE ON THE MOUNTAIN
18. I'LL FLY AWAY

Featuring the vocal talents of:

**MARK LOWRY, JEFF EASTER, MARTY FUNDERBURK,
CYNTHIA CLAWSON, JEFF STEELE, DIONNE GARDNER and JASON CRABB**

Available from your favorite music retailer, or
Daywind Records by calling 1-800-635-9581